's

CHESHIRE

by
JOHN N. MERRILL

Maps and photographs by John N. Merrill.

a J.N.M. PUBLICATION

1990

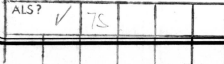

a J.N.M. PUBLICATION,

J.N.M. PUBLICATIONS,
WINSTER,
MATLOCK,
DERBYSHIRE.
DE4 2DQ
℡ Winster (062988) 454
Fax: Winster (062988) 416

Concieved, edited, typeset, designed, paged, marketed and distributed by John N. Merrill.

© Text and routes - John N. Merrill 1990.

© Maps, sketches and photographs - John N. Merrill 1990.

First Published - February 1990

ISBN 0 907496 85 7

Meticulous research has been undertaken to ensure that this publication is highly accurate at the time of going to press. The publishers, however, cannot be held responsible for alterations, errors or omissions, but they would welcome notification of such for future editions.

Typeset in - Bookman - bold, italic and plain 9pt and 18pt.

Printed by -   Elgar Printing Ltd., Hereford.

Cover photograph by John N. Merrill - Walking in Delamere Forest - "Beech Avenue".

ABOUT
JOHN N. MERRILL

John combines the characteristics and strength of a mountain climber with the stamina and athletic capabilities of a marathon runner. In this respect he is unique and has to his credit a whole string of remarkable long walks. He is without question the world's leading marathon walker.

Over the last fifteen years he has walked more than 100,000 miles and successfully completed ten walks of a least 1,000 miles or more. His six major walks in Great Britain are -

Hedridean Journey....... 1,003 miles.
Northern Isles Journey......913 miles.
Irish Island Journey ....1,578 miles.
Parkland Journey.......2,043 miles.
Land's End to John o' Groats.....1,608 miles.

and in 1978 he became the first person (permanent Guinness Book of Records entry) to walk the entire coastline of Britain - 6,824 miles in ten months.

In Europe he has walked across Austria - 712 miles - hiked the Tour of Mont Blanc, completed High Level Routes in the Dolomites and Italian Alps, and the GR20 route across Corsica in training! In 1982 he walked across Europe - 2,806 miles in 107 days - crossing seven countries, the Swiss and French Alps and the complete Pyrennean chain - the hardest and longest mountain walk in Europe, with more than 600,000 feet of ascent!

In America he used The Appalachian Trail - 2,200 miles - as a training walk, He has walked from Mexico to Canada via the Pacific Crest Trail in record time - 118 days for 2,700 miles. He has walked most of the Continental Divide Trail and much of New Mexico; his second home. In Canada he has walked the Rideau Trail - Kingston to Ottowa - 220 miles and The Bruce Trail - Tobermory to Niagara Falls - 460 miles.

In 1984 John set off from Virginia Beach on the Atlantic coast, and walked 4,226 miles without a rest day, across the width of America to Santa Cruz and San Francisco on the Pacific coast. His walk is unquestionably his greatest achievement, being, in modern history, the longest, hardest crossing of the U.S.A. in the shortest time - under six months (178 days). The direct distance is 2,800 miles.

Between major walks John is out training in his own area - The Peak District National Park. He has walked all of our National Trails many times - The Cleveland Way thirteen times and The Pennine Way four times in a year! He has been trekking in the Himalayas five times. He created more than a dozen challenge walks which have been used to raise more than £250,000 for charity. From his own walks he has raised over £100,000. He is author of more than one hundred walking guides; most of which he publishes himself, His book sales are in excess of 2 1/2 million, He has created many long distance walks including The Limey Way , The Peakland Way, Dark Peak Challenge walk, and Rivers' Way. He lectures extensively in Britain and America.

CONTENTS

MAP KEY

 - Car Park

 - Tourist Information Centre

 - Cafè

 - Railway Station

 - Nature Reserve

 - Camping site

 - Market Cross

 - Map

 - Route

 - Bridleway

 - National Trail Sign

 - Farm

 - Bus Station

 - Church

 - Public Telephone

 - House

 - Inn

 - Bed & Breakfast

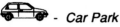 - Animal Sanctuary

- Bird Sanctuary

 - Castle

 - Historical Building

 - Abbey/Monastery

 - Bank

 - Snack Bar

 - Restaurant

 - View Point

 - Cricket Field

 - Foot-bridge

 - Steps

- Ladder Stile

- Stile

- Gate

- Trig Point

 - Hotel

 - Post Office

- Footpath Sign

- Camping Barn

- Youth Hostel

- Hospital

5

INTRODUCTION

I have spent many pleasant days walking and exploring the varied scenery encompassed in the county. The variety is astonishing from the western edge of the Peak District where it is rugged and remote to the plain; which although relatively flat is blessed by attractive villages, historic buildings and delightful woodland. Running down the western side is the magnificent Sandstone Trail following a truly splendid escarpment which is a constant delight to walk. And, as they rightly say - you are never far from a canal in Cheshire. As a result there are a few walks on them - one of the delights of walking in Britain.

My aim has been simple but hard to put into practice for there is endless scope! Simply I have endeavoured to illustrate the very varied walking in the county and at the same time get an even coverage throughout. As a result you have wood and forest walks; canal walks; sandstone ridge walking; moorland walking and walks that explore some of the village and towns of Cheshire. Helsby Hill is stunning walking; the Peckford Hills are breathtaking; Delamere Forest is a haven; Peover a forgotten gem; and Audlem a canal setting hard to equal. These are some of my favourites.

Don't hesitate to get your boots out and set off on one of these walks and explore on foot this remarkable county. I hope you enjoy them as much as I have and may I wish you
.........Happy Walking!

John N. Merrill.

ABOUT
THE WALKS

Whilst every care is taken detailing and describing the walks in this book, it should be borne in mind that the countryside changes by the seasons and the work of man. I have described the walks to the best of my ability, detailing what I have found on the walk in the way of stiles and signs. Obviously with the passage of time stiles become broken or replaced by a ladder stile or even a small gate. Signs too have a habit of being broken or pushed over. All the routes follow rights of way and only on rare occasions will you have to overcome obstacles in its path, such as a barbed wire fence or electric fence.

The seasons bring occasional problems whilst out walking which should also be borne in mind. In the height of summer paths become overgrown and you will have to fight your way through in a few places. In low lying areas the fields are often full of crops, and although the pathline goes straight across it may be more practical to walk round the field edge to get to the next stile or gate. In summer the ground is generally dry but in autumn and winter, especially because of our climate, the surface can be decidedly wet and slippery; sometimes even gluttonous mud!

These comments are part of countryside walking which help to make your walk more interesting or briefly frustrating. Standing in a farm-yard up to your ankles in mud might not be funny at the time but upon reflection was one of the highlights of the walk!

The mileage for each walk is based on three calculations -

1. pedometer reading.
2. the route map measured on the map.
3. the time I took for the walk.

I believe the figure stated for each walk to be very accurate but we all walk differently and not always in a straight line! The time allowed for each walk is on the generous side and does not include pub stops etc. The figure is based on the fact that on average a person walks 2 1/2 miles an hours but less in hilly terrain.

BEACON HILL & HELSBY HILL — 8 miles

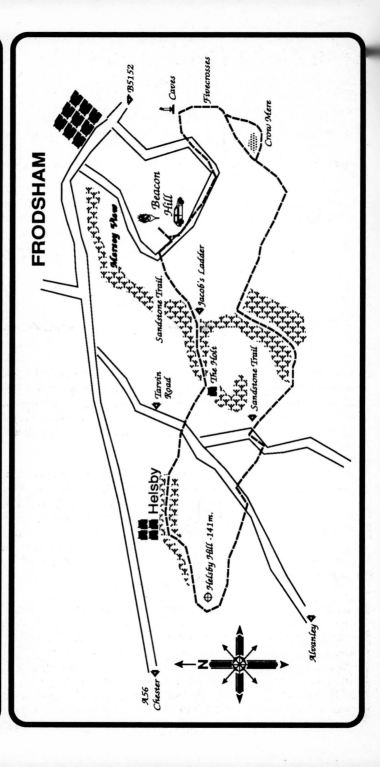

BEACON HILL & HELSBY HILL
- 8 miles
- allow 3 hours.

••• •• •• -*Beacon Hill Car Park - Sandstone Trail - Tarvin Road - Helsby - Helsby Hill - Sandstone Trail - Snidley Moor - Dobers Lane - Crow Mere - Fivecrosses - Beacon Hill.*

 - *O.S. 1:25,000 Pathfinder Series Sheet No. 757 (SJ 47/57) -Ellesmere Port (East).*

- *Beacon Hill at Grid Ref.: SJ 518766.*

- *None on the walk. Nearest just off the route at Fivecrosses.*

ABOUT THE WALK - One of the longest in the book but this is of little consequence for the walk is outstanding. The scenery of woodland and sandstone outcrops and the extensive views over the Mersey and North Wales combine to make this walk a very memorable one indeed. Take your time and savour one of the finest walks in Cheshire!

WALKING INSTRUCTIONS - From the car park return to the road and turn right. In a few yards turn left at the Sandstone Trail footpath sign - Manley Common/Delamere Forest. Descend the track to a stile and continue ahead crossing Frodsham Golf Course. At the end reach a stile and steps at the start of woodland and the sandstone outcrop. Instead of descending the steps to the base of the cliffs you can continue basically ahead and descend Jacob's Ladder - a footpath cut out of the rock.

At the base of the cliffs descend to a Mid Cheshire Footpath Society Sign and bear left following the path signed - Helsby. The path ascends past more cliffs to the wood's edge where you turn sharp right and ascend a sandstone outcrop. The path now keeps to the upper edge of the wood and in less than 1/2 reach a Sandstone Trail sign and path veering left. You keep straight ahead along the top of the cliffs to the wood's end. Here you turn right and descend through the wood on a good path to the entrance gates to The Holt. Descend the drive to Tarvin Road. Here turn left then right onto a road "unsuitable for Motors" and in 1/4 mile reach a ford where the road turns right. Leave the road here and ascend to the steps to a stile. Cross the field to a footbridge and continue along a hedged path to a lane. Go straight across this as stiled and bear right across the field to a stile and another path between the houses to Bates Lane. Here turn right then left along Old Chester Road in Helsby.

After a few yards and on the right of Holly Cottage - No 25 - turn left up the signed footpath. Pass through a stile and continue ascending to another and turn right into National Trust property - Helsby Hill. In a few yards take the lefthand path and again a few yards later. You are following the upper path that leads to the triangulation pillar on the summit of the hill. The views from here are incredible. Follow the path leftwards from the trig pillar, away from the edge, following the edge of the field; it is well used. Gain the end of track via a stile and turn left along it. It soon becomes tarmaced. First it bears right then left and shortly afterwards is the stile and footpath sign on your right - Tarvin Road/Commonside.

Keep to the edge of the field to a ladder stile where you turn left and cross the field to the far righthand corner to a stile and walled track. Follow this round to a minor road and path sign - Hill Road. Turn left and in about 75 yards turn right at the stile and footpath sign. First you keep the field boundary on your right to a stile and footbridge, then on your left to a minor road, gained by a stile by a pathsign. Turn left down Burrows Lane to the T junction. Turn right and in less than 1/4 mile turn left onto a track, back onto the Sandstone Trail and signposted - Woodhouse Hill.

Keep on this track/path for the next 3/4 mile. In more than 1/4 mile you enter woodland and continue ascending gently and ignoring any branch trails until you reach the top and wood perimeter infront of you, The Sandstone Trail goes to your left but you turn right and follow an ascending track out of the wood and follow it for the next 1/2 mile to Manley Road. Go straight across and continue on a track and in 1/4 mile reach Dobers Lane. Turn left along the lane to the road junction beside Crow Mere. You can continue straight ahead but I prefer to turn right and follow the path which is signposted. Past the mere it turns left and is mostly a fenced path. As you descend you pass a small wooded area before emerging onto the road by a path sign.

Turn right and in a few yards left past the houses of Fivecrosses, passing en route Marling House on your left. A little further and where the road turns right by House No 24 turn left to the stile and footpath sign. Ascend the field to the top righthand corner keeping to the left of the childrens play area. Pass through the stile and follow the path close to the field edge past an impressive sandstone outcrop once occupied by a hermit. Descend to the road, stile and path sign. Turn left and in a few yards right following the road to Mersey View. In 1/4 mile you are back at Beacon Hill and the car park on your right.

THE SANDSTONE TRAIL - 32 miles long from Beacon Hill along the sandstone escarpment in Cheshire to Grindley Brook, in the south. Developed by the Cheshire County Council and similar to the Gritstone Trail it has a walking boot imprint with the letter S waymarking the route. It is usually done in a north to south direction, and is highly recommended. Several other walks touch sections of the route such as the Beeston walk.

Cliff face of Helsby Hill

LYME PARK & BOW STONES
- 4 miles

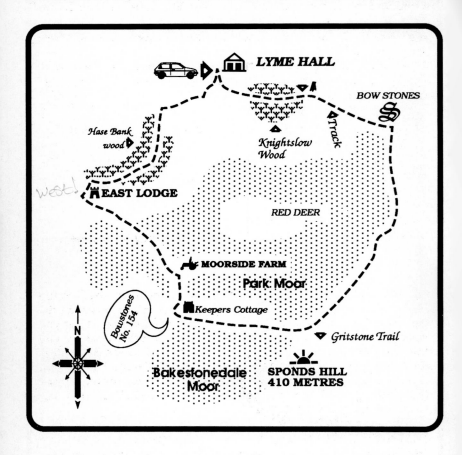

LYME HALL - dates back to the 16th century, with a splendid Elizabethan long gallery. Originally it was the home of the Legh family, but this century passed to the National Trust. The palladian front dates from the 18th century. Among the treasures are Grinling Gibbons carvings and relics associated with Charles Stuart.

LYME PARK & BOW STONES
- 4 miles
- allow 1 1/2 hours.

▄▖ ▖▄ ▄▖ - *Lyme Hall Car Park - Knott Gate - Hase Bank Wood - West Lodge - Keepers Cottage - Dale Top - Sponds Hill - Bow Stones - Gritstone Trail - Lyme Hall Car Park.*

 - *O.S. 1:25,000 Pathfinder Series Sheet No. 741 (SJ 88/98) - Stockport (South).*

🚗 - *Lyme Hall. Grid Ref. SJ 964824.*

🍾 - *None on the walk - sorry!*
Refreshments available near Lyme Hall. Nearest inns in Disley.

ABOUT THE WALK - Is a jewel to the south of Stockport. The impressive hall (National Trust property) is well worth a visit as are the gardens. The walk starts and ends at the hall's car park. First you walk through Hase Bank Wood to West Lodge. Just after you ascend into moorland , gradually, to near the summit of Sponds Hill, 410m. Extensive views all the way as you follow the Gritstone Trail to Bow Stones. Here you descend , still following the trail, through Lyme Park to the car park. En route you have views to the hall and no doubt hear and see the red deer herd.

WALKING INSTRUCTIONS - From the car park walk westwards (to your right) on the tarmaced road and soon pass a little to your left the Gritstone Trail pathsign. It down here you will be returning. Continue on the road and take the left fork and follow it down into a hollow to Knott Gate at the entrance to Hase Bank Wood. Go through the gate and keep on the track for the next 1/2 mile along the floor of the wood to West Lodge. Here turn left along the track to Shrigley Road. Bear left along it and in a few yards just on the right of the Methodist Church turn left along the track signposted Green Close Farm.

Keep on the track ascending past the houses where it becomes a path. For the 3/4 mile you ascend moorland keeping the boundary wall of Lyme Park on your left. Approaching Moorside Farm the path bears right to a stile and Moorside Lane. By the stile is path sign No. 155 - Higher Poynton. Turn right and in a few yards pass Keepers Cottage on your left. On its righthand side turn left by footpath sign No. 154 - Bow Stones. Follow the path by the wall for just over 1/2 mile to crest of the moorland, near Dale Top, to a stile. Bear left and follow the defined path close to the boundary wall of Lyme Park. In more than 1/2 mile gain a stile and track close to Sponds Hill on your right.

Turn left and walk along the track, now following the Gritstone Trail, and in less than 1/2 mile reach the end of a tarmaced lane via a stile. Just ahead is the Bow Stones. Before them and on the left of the entrance to Bowstones Farm is a stile and path sign - Lyme Park. Now you descend to a ladder stile and reenter Lyme Park. The track is well defined down through moorland for 1/2 mile to another ladder stile. Ascend this and enter Knightslow Wood. Keep to the track though the wood ignoring any side branches to another ladder stile. Ascend this and turn right walking beside woodland and descending to the gate and Gritstone Trail sign you passed at the start. Bear right to the car park.

GRITSTONE TRAIL - Starts beside the hall and traverses the final gritstone hills above the Cheshire Plain for 18 1/2 miles to Rushton Spencer and the Staffordshire Way.

BOW STONES - Two Saxon cross shafts believed to mark the boundary of Macclesfield Forest.

Lyme Hall

DELAMERE FOREST - 6 miles

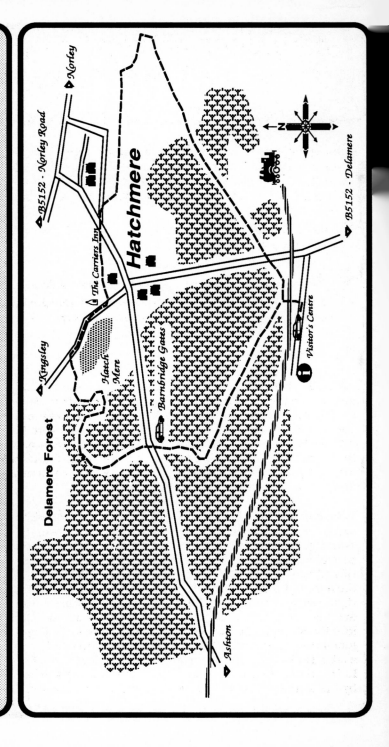

DELAMERE FOREST - 6 miles
- allow 2 1/2 hours.

•● ●● •● - *Visitor's Centre Car Park - Delamere Forest - Norley path - Harthill Bank - Hatchmere - Flaxmere - The Carriers Inn - Hatch Mere - Delamere Forest - Barnbridge Gates - Visitor's Centre Car Park.*

- O.S. 1:25,000 Pathfinder Series Sheet No. 757 (SJ 47/57) - Ellesmere Port (East).

- By Visitor's Centre, just off the Delamere Road - B5152 - at Grid Ref.: SJ 549704. Further car park at Barnbridge Gate - Grid Ref.: SJ 543705 - which the walk passes.

- The Carriers Inn, Hatchmere.

ABOUT THE WALK - Delamere Forest is an exceptional walking area with a lattice work of paths to choose from. This walk explores the forest and surrounding area taking you to many of the key places and serves as a curtain raiser for exploring on your own. For the ornithologist the forest has much to offer. The walk starts and ends at the Visitor's Centre car park; a visit to the centre and adjoining displays adds greatly to your appreciation and understanding of the area,

WALKING INSTRUCTIONS - Walk out of the Car Park to your left to sign - Forest Walks - and turn left over the bridge over the railway. Turn right immediately and descend steps into the wood. Keep to the path along the forest's perimeter and in less than 1/2 mile reach the B5152 road. Cross over to the track and footpath sign - Norley. For the next 1/4 mile the track is well defined with a small lake on your right. When you approach the forest perimeter ignore the turning left and keep ahead. For the next 1/2 mile ignore all branch paths by keeping straight ahead. Nearing the end of the forest you reach a junction of three trails; take the middle one and in a few yards gain a stile. Here you leave the forest behind and follow a defined track . In less than 1/4 mile it turns right; leave it at the stile on your left by the footpath sign and follow the path around Harthill Bank.

Reach another stile and solitary oak tree beyond. Bear left and follow a path which soon ascends to the field edge on your left. Walk beside it to a stile and to another. The track descends but in a few yards turn left at a stile and walk along the righthand side of the field to a stile. Continue along the field edge to the next field and bear right; not into the farm but to the righthand edge of the field and its top righthand corner is a stile.

Over the stile turn left along Post Office Road to the junction with School Lane. Go straight across and follow a No Through Road keeping to the lefthand branch and passing a house built in 1833, where you follow a path to a track and at the end of which is the B5152 and The Carriers Inn. Turn right and on your left is Hatch Mere. In less than 1/4 mile along the road turn left just past the end of the mere onto a footpath - before the Petrol Station. You keep on this path for the next 1/2 mile as you almost encircle the mere but in woodland. Upon reaching a footbridge cross it and bear right into Delamere Forest proper and gain a wide track after a stile. Turn right along it . Keep on it for the next 1/4 mile to the next junction where you bear right and in more than 1/4 mile reach the forest's perimeter with a lake full of rotting trees on your left. Turn left and follow the track through the forest ignoring all side trails and in a 1/3 mile reach the minor road with Barnbridge Gates Car Park opposite. En route you will joined the Sandstone Trail.

Cross to the right of the car park, Trail signed, and continue passing a notice board to the trail on your left. Just after is a path sign - Visitor's Centre 2 km (1.2 miles). Continue on the track to a solitary table where you bear right and walk along a splendid avenue of beech trees. At the next footpath junction turn left; signed posted Visitor's Centre. The track you now follow is a cycle route as well. Keep on this through the forest ignoring all turnings and in less than a mile cross the railway bridge you crossed at the beginning of the walk. Turn right back to the car park.

DELAMERE FOREST - a former Royal Forest and James 1st was the last monarch to hunt here. The forest covers 2,400 acres and is a mixture of pine and hardwoods. The forest is a major ornithologist observation area with a wide variety of birds to be seen. Grey Squirrels are predominant and red foxes are often sighted.

Delamere Forest - Beech avenue, near Barnbridge Gates.

FORESTRY COMMISSION

DELAMERE FOREST

Horse Riding by permit only

Cycling on authorised cycle route only

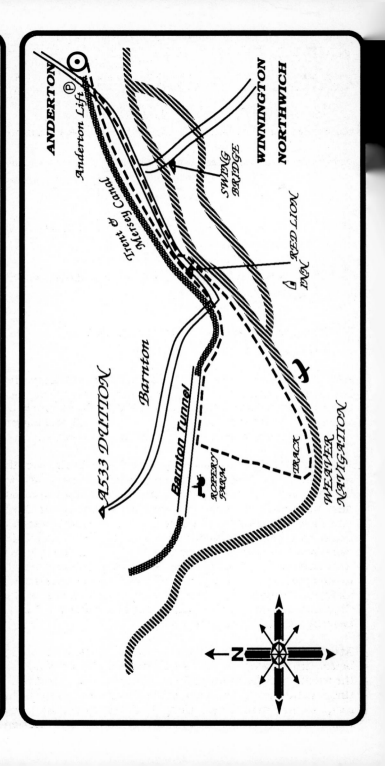

ANDERTON, TRENT & MERSEY CANAL & WEAVER NAVIGATION
- 3 miles. - allow 1 1/4 hours.

•► •_ •► - *Anderton Lift - Trent & Mersey Canal - Barnton*
Tunnel - Weaver Navigation - Anderton Lift.

- *O.S. 1:25,000 Pathfinder Series Sheet No. 758 (SJ 67/77)*
- *Northwich & Knutsford.*

- *No official one but parking space opposite Anderton Lift*
at Grid Ref. SJ 647753.

- *Stanley Arms, Anderton near start of walk.*
Red Lion Inn 2 miles around the walk.

ABOUT THE WALK - The Anderton Lift that transported boats between the Trent & Mersey Canal and the Weaver Navigation is one of the finest artifacts of the canal age. This walk enables you to walk along both waterways and appreciate the skill and endeavour of man. Take your time and explore the timeless setting.

WALKING INSTRUCTIONS - Cross the footbridge over the Trent & Mersey Canal opposite the Anderton Lift and turn right following the tow path, with the canal on your right. Follow the canal for the next mile mostly through woodland and passing canal milepost - Shardlow 86 miles/Preston Brook 6 miles . Shortly after the canal bears right then left to the entrance of the Barnton Tunnel. Leave the canal hear and ascend the path above it and in 100 yards reach a wooden stile in the hedge on your left. Ascend this and cross the field to the lefthand side of Ropery Farm where there is a stile. Continue along the field edge using the stiles to a gate before a hedged track. Continue ahead along this bearing right soon along it. The track can be overgrown in summer in places.

At the end of the track reach the Weaver Navigation. Turn left walking beside the Barnton Cut and follow the path for the next 3/4 mile to the track which leads to the Red Lion Inn on your left. You can continue further along the Weaver but there is no access to the A533 road. At the inn turn right along the A533 road to the swing bridge over the Weaver. Keep straight ahead on the ascending road and just before it crosses the canal turn right on the path and rejoin your starting out path and follow it to your right to the Anderton Lift. A cobbled path on the right leads down to the wharf and gives a clearer view of the lift.

THE ANDERTON BOAT LIFT - Was opened in 1875 and is in all probability the finest piece of canal engineering in Britain today. Prior to its construction there was considerable trade on the Trent & Mersey Canal and the River Weaver., fifty feet below; especially salt. Goods were manhandled between the two and shoots were built to slide the salt down, but it was still very labour intensive. The lift was originally hydraulically operated. A canal boat entered the top of the lift in its own water, into a watertight tank. Another boat on the River Weaver would enter a similar tank and by releasing a small amount of water to make the upper tank heavier, the boats would descend and rise, passing each other. The tanks are 75 feet long by 15 feet 6 ins wide and fully loaded with water weighed 252 tons. In 1908 the lift was converted to electrical power and 250 ton counterweights were added; and the whole structure was strengthened. Plans are underway to totally restore the lift to working order and build a Visitor's Centre.

NORTHWICH - The town's coat of arms says - "Sal est Vita", meaning Salit is Life. Salt has been mined here since Roman times.

Trent & Mersey Canal at Anderton Boat Lift.

The Anderton Boat Lift

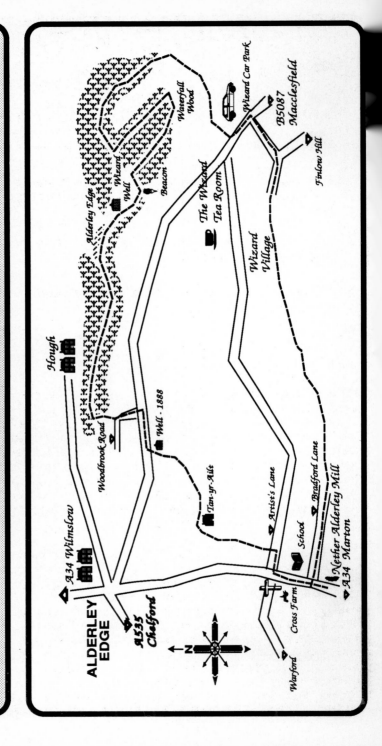

ALDERLEY EDGE
- 6 miles - allow 2 1/2 hours.

•◦ ◦• •◦ *- Alderley Edge Car Park - Edge House Farm - Clock House Wood - Waterfall Wood - Alderley Edge - Armada Beacon - Wizard's Well -White Barn Farm - Nether Alderley Cross & Mill - Bradford Lane - Car Park.*

📖 *- O.S. 1:25,000 Pathfinder Series Sheet No. SJ 87/97*
  - Macclesfield & Alderley Edge.

🚗 *- On the B5087 road near The Wizard Restaurant.*
  Grid Ref. SJ 859773.

🍾 *-None on the walk but tea room at The Wizard.*
  Inns in downtown Alderley Edge.

ABOUT THE WALK - Alderley Edge - National Trust property - is a magnificent walking area through woodland and rocky outcrops providing extensive views over northern Cheshire. It is rich on folklore and legend. The walk takes a lengthy meandering route through woodland before skirting Alderley Edge village to Nether Alderley where there is a remarkable cross base. Just off the route but well worth visiting is Nether Alderley Mill, National Trust Property. You return to the car park via a bridleway - Bradford Lane. Autumn is a particularly fine time to walk here to appreciate the fall colours.

WALKING INSTRUCTIONS - From the car park leave it at its northern end and follow the path towards The Wizard's Tea Room. Turn right along the track passing the Foresters Lodge on your left. The track bears left but leave it on your right at a stile and follow a fenced path down the field away from the trees. Continue past Edge House Farm keeping to the well stiled path which soon turns right then left as you follow a track to a stream crossing. On your left is a path into Waterfall Wood -you will be walking in here soon. Keep to the fields by bearing right on a fenced path to a stile. Then turn left beside the fence before turning right passing two small ponds on your left and gain a track on the wood's edge. On your right is Hill Top.

Turn left and enter the woodland and National Trust Property. The track descends through Clock House Wood to near Clock House Farm. Here you keep straight ahead in woodland keeping to the defined path.

The path soon bears left and you follow it keeping to the lefthand edge of the woodland and enter Waterfall Wood. Keep to the lefthand edge of the wood and follow the path up the small gorge to the top of the waterfall - often dry. Turn right across the top and continue close to the lefthand side of the wood as you follow the path round to your left into Dickens Wood - part of the time you are just outside the wood. Bear right along a track to a junction of tracks. Take the right one - a really wide avenue and suitable for wheelchairs and in 1/4 mile reach the main outcrop of rock of Alderley Edge with its fine views. The track bears left but leave via the path which soon bears left and swings right and ascends to the memorial on the site of the Armada Beacon. Continue along the lefthand edge of the woodland passing rocky outcrops. Descend to the path at the base of the edge and reach the Wizard's Well. Just after keep to the lefthand path and reach a stile. Turn left and gain Woodbrook Road. Descend it to the B5087 road.

Turn right and pass Tempest Road on your right. Just after turn left onto a footpath between the houses - there is a small well in the wall on the left dated 1888. The path is well defined and after the stile at the end bear right keeping a high wall on your right to another stile. Over this you keep close to a fence and reach a further stile and road. Turn right past the large houses and after the fourth one on your left - Tan-yr-Ailt - turn left as footpath signed - Nether Alderley. At first it is a fenced path then you emerge into fields but all the time you keep to the perimeter fence of the houses on your right, en route passing two stiles. In 1/2 mile reach a minor road -Artists Lane - and turn right to the A34 road opposite the base of Nether Alderley cross.

Turn left along the road and in 150 yards pass the school on your left and Bradford Lane. You turn left up here but it worth walking a little further to see Nether Alderley Mill. Walk up Bradford Lane which for much of it is cobbled. In 1/2 mile pass Bradford House and continue on the track passing Wizard Village on your left. Afterwards it becomes a metalled surface. At the road junction turn left to the B5087 road. Turn left along this road and in a few yards the car park is on your right.

THE WIZARD'S WELL -   above the well are the carved words -
"Drink of this and take thy fill,
For the water falls by the wizard's will."

The Wizard's Well   *The Wizard Restaurant sign.*

THE WIZARD OF ALDERLEY EDGE - according to the legend the wizard lived near the well. One day he spoke to a farmer going to Macclesfield market with a white horse to sell. The wizard offered him a price but was refused. But no one bought it and upon his return the wizard led him to a rock. Whereupon it opened showing King Arthur and his knights asleep. The wizard said they were a white horse short and offered the farmer some gold for it. The farmer who was now speechless took the gold and fled. Since then no-one has seen the cave where King Arthur lay asleep.

Nether Alderley Mill

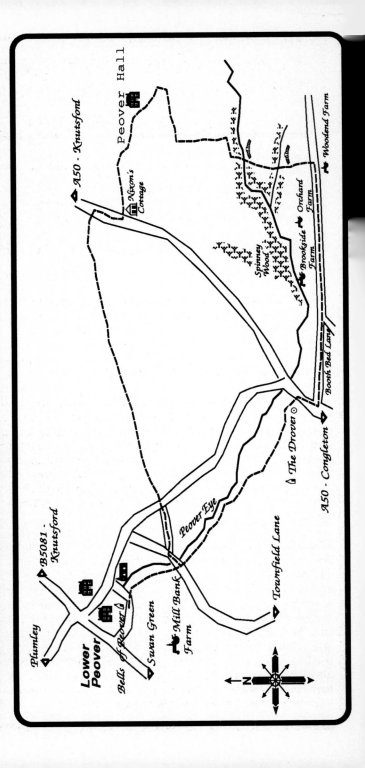

LOWER PEOVER & PEOVER HALL - 7 miles
- allow 2 1/2 hours.

⬤▪ ▪⬤ ⬤▪ - *Lower Peover - Peover Eye - The Drover's Inn - A50 - Booth Bed Lane - Woodend Farm - Peover Hall - Holmes Chapel Road (A50) - Hillcrest Farm - Mill Bank Farm - Lower Peover.*

O.S. 1:25,000 Pathfinder Series Sheet No. 758 - (SJ 67/77) - Northwich & Knutsford.

- No official one. The walk starts and ends at Lower Peover church, Grid Ref. SJ 743742.

- Bells of Peover at Lower Peover.
   The Drover's Inn on the A50 road.

ABOUT THE WALK - An absolutely fascinating area with good footpaths and well stiled. Lower Peover with its cobbled street and cluster of houses is a gem. The church is of particular note. You cross fields and beside the meandering Peover Eye to the A50. Past this you are back in delightful quiet countryside with views to Jodrell Bank. Crossing woodland you gain the magnificent Peover Hall, set in extensive gardens. You return over the fields back to the Peover Eye and retrace your starting out steps back to Lower Peover; a real gem of a walk.

WALKING INSTRUCTIONS - Walk along "The Cobbles" in Lower Peover and follow the path along the righthand side of the church to a kissing gate. Follow the defined path ahead which soon curves right and in 1/4 mile reach the Peover Eye on your left. Continue to a stiles and a lane. Cross over to another stile and continue walking close to the river on your left. After two more stiles you leave the riverside and walk beside a fence on your right to the end of the field to another stile. Here turn right and at the end of the field left at the stile. Keep the hedge on your right and gain four more stiles. After the last one aim for the far righthand corner of the field to a gate. Through this turn left and walk around the field edge to a gate beside a pathsign - Lower Peover. On your left is the Drover's Inn.

Turn right beside the A50 road for 1/4 to the first road on your left - Booth Bed Lane. Turn left along this and where it turns right beside The Smithy, keep straight ahead on another lane, a No Through Road. You keep on this lane for the next 3/4 mile passing Brookside Farm and Orchard Farm. The lane becomes a track as you reach Woodend Farm on your right. Just past it on your left is a footpath sign; turn left and walk along the field edge to a gate and enter woodland. Cross a footbridge and emerge from the woodland. Turn left and walk around the field just inside a fence. Well round the other side follow the path into woodland and a large footbridge over the Peover Eye. Keep straight ahead and ascend out of the woodland to a gate. Turn right beside the wood's edge before turning right along a track to the road to Peover Hall. Turn right and in 50 yards turn left along the road following the signs for Peover Church, en route passing through Home Farm.

At the entrance to the church turn left on a path through the trees to a wider path and follow this across the grounds to a stile near the estate wall. Turn left to another stile and cross the subsequent field aiming for the righthand corner 1/4 mile away of the wood on your left. Bear left keeping the wood on your lefthand reach the A50 road by a footpath sign - Over Peover Church. On your left is an attractive thatched cottage - Nixon's Cottage. Turn right and in a few yards turn left onto a track - footpath signed - and follow this to Hillcrest Farm. Enter the farm and turn left then right and mostly keep to a track along the righthand edge of the field. At the end bear right to a stile and continue with the hedge on your right to reach another. After this you cross an open field, aiming for the left of the houses to a track and path sign. Turn right then left immediately and follow the lane to its junction 1/4 mile away. Turn left and cross the Peover Eye and turn right at the stile by the path sign on your right and retrace your steps back to Lower Peover.

PEOVER HALL - Family home of the Mainwarings. The hall was built in 1585 and the church is dedicated to St. Lawrence.

LOWER PEOVER - The church tower is 16th century but the timbered aisles are 14th century.

Lower Peover church.

Peover Hall.

BEESTON AND WASTE HILL
- 4 1/2 miles

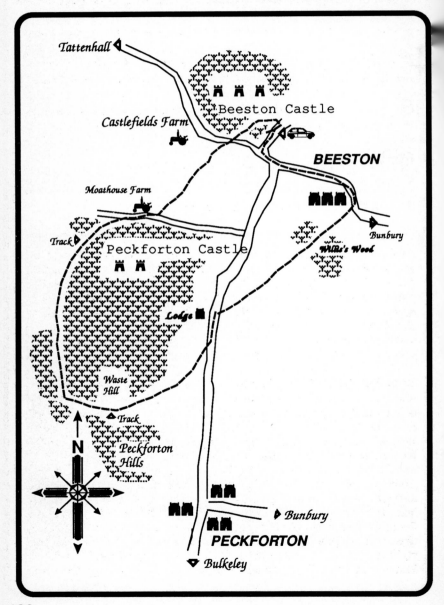

Tattenhall

Beeston Castle

Castlefields Farm

BEESTON

Moathouse Farm

Bunbury

Track

Peckforton Castle

Wilkie's Wood

Lodge

Waste
Hill

Track

N

Peckforton
Hills

Bunbury

PECKFORTON

Bulkeley

BEESTON AND WASTE HILL
- 4 1/2 miles
- allow 2 hours.

`•• •• ••` - *Beeston Castle - Moathouse Farm - Peckforton Hills Waste Hill - East Lodge - Willis's Wood - Beeston - Beeston Castle.*

 - 0.5. 1:25,000 Pathfinder Series Sheet No SJ 45/55 Farndon, Holt and Tattenhall.

- Beeston Castle. Grid Ref. SJ 540589.

- Sorry - there is no inn on this walk!

ABOUT THE WALK - Absolutely stunning! Beeston Castle and the wooded Peckforton Hills erupt from the Cheshire Plain providing 360 degree views to the Peak District, the Mersey, and north Wales. The paths are all well defined and stiled and pass through mature woodlands, which are a joy to walk through. If time permits a visit to Beeston Castle is very rewarding, historically, and also to see where you have walked! The route follows a section of the Sandstone Trail and the yellow footprint sign will be seen.

WALKING INSTRUCTIONS - From the car park entrance turn sharp left onto the wooded fenced path, as signposted. The path soon descends through pine trees to a minor road. Cross over to your left to the well defined path across a field. In August when I was walking the route the field was full of ripening corn. Gain a stile and cross a footbridge to another stile. Continue ahead ascending gently to another minor road, by a stile and path sign Bulkeley Hill - a sign name you will see often along the first half of the route. Turn right along the road and soon pass Moathouse Farm on your right. A little later turn left at a gate by the path sign - Bulkeley Hill - and enter Peckforton Wood. Follow the well defined track for 1/2 mile, close to the wood's edge in the latter stages to a cross roads of paths - on your right is a small farm. Continue ahead on the signed path - Bulkeley Hill and in 1/4 mile at the next simarily named sign leave the track and ascend the path up the slope. At the top by path sign - Hill Lane - by a stile continue ahead in open country on a defined path to another stile. Beyond this reach another and gain Hill Lane.

Turn left and soon begin descending down the track from Waste Hill. In 1/4 mile pass under a bridge and follow the track slightly to your left and reach a gate. Just after turn left to the path and sign - Beeston. The path keeps to the field edge on your left before gaining a stile and you start descending to two more stiles. The path is defined as you continue over the field brow and descend to two more stiles and gain a minor road by apath sign. Turn left along the Peckforton/Beeston road for little over 1/4 mile to the East Lodge of Peckforton Castle. Here on the right is the stile and path sign - Beeston. The path line is undefined but simply bear left across the large field aiming towards the lefthand side of Willis's Wood a 1/3 mile away. Gain the stile and follow the path through the wood to another stile. Over this pass a small pond on your left and cross another large field aiming for the righthand side of Brook Farm. Here is another stile. Over this continue across a track and follow another to the minor road and path sign - Peckforton. Turn left along the lane through Beeston village. Keep left at the road junction and right at the next, following the signs for Beeston Castle. Turn left almost immediately to reach the car park beneath Beeston Castle.

BEESTON CASTLE - Building began in 1220 by the sixth Earl of Chester, Ranulf de Blundeville. In the 14th century it became a Royal castle and extensive alterations were made to the towers and the construction of a drawbridge. It is said that Richard 11 hid his jewels and treasure here but despite frequent searching nothing has been found. In the 16th century the castle was in poor condition and in 1642/3 during the Civil War and saw several battles during this period. By 1646 the castle was "Pulled downe and utterlie defaced." The ruins belong to the Tollemache family.

PECKFORTON CASTLE – Known as the "other castle" it was built for John Tollemache between 1842 - 1851. It is built to 15th century design and is reputed to have cost £70,000. Lord Bentley Tollemache lived here until 1939 and since then it has been little used.

Peckforton Castle and path to Moathouse Farm.

Beeston Castle from path to Moathouse Farm.

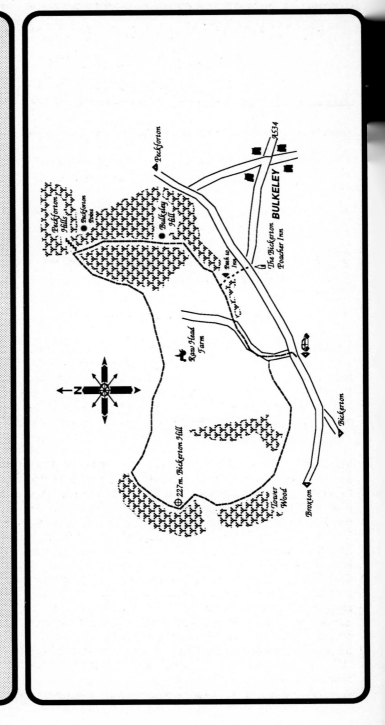

BICKERTON HILL & BULKELEY HILL - 4 1/2 miles
- allow 2 hours.

 - *Bickerton Hill - Bulkeley Hill - Grig Hill Farm - Little Heath - Raw Head - Tower Wood - Bickerton-hill.*

- *O.S. 1:25,000 Pathfinder Series Sheet No.SJ 45/55 - Farndon, Holt and Tattenhall.*

- *Opposite road junction to hamlet of Bickerton Hill - Grid Ref. SJ 518542.*

-- *The Bickerton Poacher inn, just off the route.*

ABOUT THE WALK - You first ascend through woodland to the summit of Bulkeley Hill with its impressive views to Peckforton Point. Next. you curve round beside woodland at first then open country to the western edge of the escarpment near Raw Head. The walk along the escarpment edge is outstanding with spectacular outcrops of sandstone. It is a walk to savour. There is no inn actually on the walk but just off it and signed is the Bickerton Poacher.

WALKING INSTRUCTIONS - From the parking area opposite the junction of the road to Bickerton-hill walk up the Bickerton-hill road. Follow it round to your right then left as it ascends. After a 1/3 mile near a No Through Road sign turn right, as path signed - Bickerton Poacher. In less than 1/4 mile pass a`stile and where the path begins to descend bear left on a path which takes you past a water trough on your left and woodland on your right. Beyond the trough keep the woodland on your right to reach a ladder stile. Turn left. on the defined track and in a few yards turn right onto another by the path sign - Bulkeley Hill. You ascend gently to the wall of a small reservoir. Continue ahead and basically keep to the crest of the hill as you contour round to Bulkeley Hill. There are several paths here which add to the confusion but by keeping to the edge you will have no problem. Continue past the "summit" on the hill's edge and in 1/4 mile the path veers away to the left from the edge before you descend steps to a track.

Turn left along the track soon passing Grig Hill Farm. The track bears right and in a 1/3 mile from the farm, on a lefthand corner in the track ascend the stile on your right and keep to the field edge to another stile and path sign - Burwardsley. Turn right onto another track passing the entrance to The Bungalow on your right. Soon pass a ruined quarry on your left and reach another stile. A little later ascend steps and gradually climb to the escarpment edge, gaining it near a rock overhang. The path is well defined as you walk along the edge to the triangulation pillar on Raw Head (Bickerton Hill). The path turns left then right as you descend steps and pass above an impressive sandstone edge. Here you bear left and slowly ascend to the lefthand edge of Tower Wood. At the end of the wood gain a track and turn left as signed - copper Mines. A few yards later bear left again following the path signed - Poacher Inn. The path descends to cross a wooded dale via a footbridge before ascending to the Bickerton-hill road, by a stile and path sign. Turn right and descend to the parking space a few yards away.

Sandstone cliffs near Raw Head.

Sandstone cliffs near Raw Head.

BICKERTON AND MAIDEN CASTLE - 3 miles

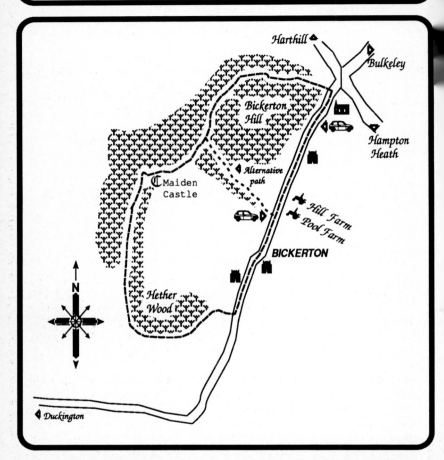

View to Raw Head from Bickerton Hill

BICKERTON AND MAIDEN CASTLE - 3 miles.
- allow 1 1/4 hours.

- Bickerton church - Bickerton Wood - Maiden Castle - Hether Wood - Bickerton - Bickerton church.

- O.S. 1:25,000 Pathfinder Series Sheet No SJ 45/55 - Farndon, Holt and Tattenhall.

- No official one but road side parking at Bickerton church - Grid Ref. SJ 509536.

- Sorry - no inn on this walk!

ABOUT THE WALK - A superb little circuit at the southern end of Bickerton Hill. Magnificent views in all directions. First you walk through woodland before gaining the heather slopes near Maiden Castle - a former Iron Age fort with 4 foot high earthworks. You contour round the fringe of Hether Wood to Bickerton village, which you walk through back to its church a mile away.

WALKING INSTRUCTIONS - Starting just west of the church at the path sign - Larkton Hill. Turn right onto the track and soon reach a stile. Continue on the defined path gradually ascending through woodland for more than 1/2 mile to a crossroads of paths. Go straight across as signed -Larkton Hill. The path keeps well to the escarpment edge and in a 1/3 mile reaches the earthworks of Maiden Castle. At the National Trust Plaque - turn right and leave the edge and descend steps to the top of of wooded valley. Continue over the other side on a defined track soon walking beside an open space on your left. In a short distance turn left on a defined path and in a few yards bear right along it as you keep close to edge of Hether Wood. Keep on this for more than 1/2 mile before bearing right down a track to the Bickerton road. Turn left and walk along the road through the scattered village for a mile back to the church, en route passing Pool Farm and Hill Farm. There is parking space opposite Pool Farm by a path onto the escarpment.

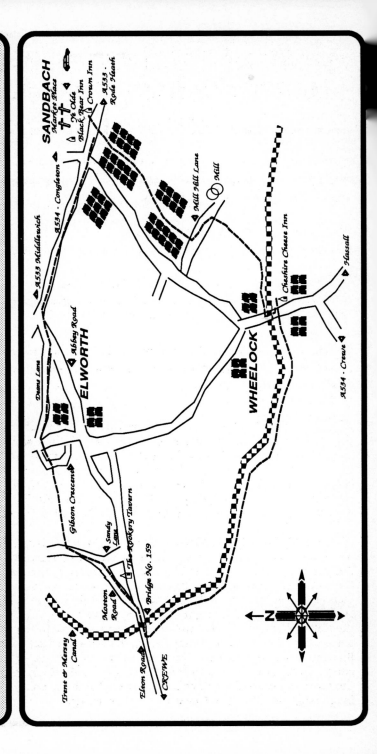

SANDBACH AND THE TRENT & MERSEY CANAL - 5 1/2 miles.

- allow 2 hours

▪▪ ▪▪ ▪▪ *- Sandbach Cross - Mill Hill Lane - Trent & Mersey Canal - Wheelock - Bridge No 159 - Elworth - Sandbach.*

📖 *- O.S. 1:25,000 Pathfinder Series Sheet Nos. 791 (SJ 65/75) - Crewe and No 775 (SJ 66/76) - Winsford (Cheshire) and Sandbach.*

🚗 *- Market Place, Sandbach - Grid Ref.: SJ758608 - restricted parking during the week but unlimited on Sunday's. Further car park to the north of the Market Place.*

🍾 *- Several in Sandbach Market Place, including The Crown and Ye Olde Bear Inn. Cheshire Cheese Inn at Wheelock and The Rookery Tavern at Ettiley Heath.*

ABOUT THE WALK - The Saxon crosses in the Market Place, where the walk begins are impressive, as is the Market Place surrounded by inns; one of the m thatched - Ye Olde Bear. The route leads from the town centre along a good path into fields and impressive mill before gaining the Trent & Mersey Canal. You follow the canal for more than two miles to Bridge No 159 near Ettiley Heath. Here it is a road walk but a pleasant one back to Sandbach Market Place.

WALKING INSTRUCTIONS - From the Market Place cross the A533 road to the path between the Victor Value and Haydens stores. For the next 1/2 mile to Mill Hill Lane you basically keep ahead on the path, which is well maintained, as it passes through housing estates. Upon reaching Mill Hill Lane turn left down it for 100 yards to the path sign on your right - Crewe Road 1/2 mile. Just ahead is the mill and on your left the mill dam. Turn right and follow the path across the mill stream and then beside it. Cross the disused railway line and continue beside the stream before crossing it and gaining the canal. Turn right along it to Bridge No 154 in Wheelock. Ascend to the road and cross the bridge to the other side of the canal - gained by passing the Cheshire Cheese Inn on your right.

Upon reaching the canal a little to your right is the canal milepost - Shardlow 69 miles/Preston Brook 23 miles. Turn left along the canal keeping it on your righthand side and walk under Bridge No 154, which is a low one. You keep beside the canal for the next two miles passing Bridge No 157 and milepost - Shardlow 70 miles/Preston Brook 22 miles. At Bridge No 159 leave the canal and cross the bridge following Elton Road. Soon pass under a railway bridge and turn left along Moston Road. You can keep ahead to The Rookery Tavern and just past it turn left along Sandy Lane and reach the junction with Moston Road. Keep left at the junction and in less than 1/4 mile where the road turns left turn right onto a grass track, signposted Gibson Crescent. Just after crossing the disused railway line turn left along Gibson Crescent. At the road junction go straight across and walk along Deans Lane. At the end turn left along Abbey Road to the A533 road. Turn right and follow this for nearly a mile back the Market Place.

SANDBACH - The two Saxon Crosses in the Market Place date from the 8th/9th century. The cobbled Market Place is particularly attractive. A large open market is held on a Thursday.

Trent & Mersey Canal at Wheelock.

Sandbach Crosses.

LITTLE MORETON HALL & TRENT & MERSEY CANAL - 10 miles

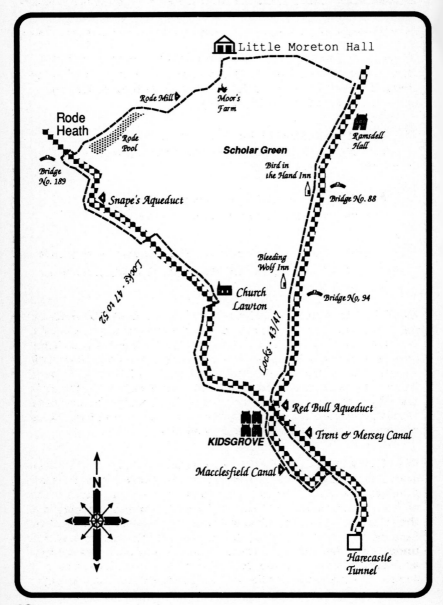

Little Moreton Hall

Rode Mill

Moor's Farm

Rode Heath

Rode Pool

Scholar Green

Ramsdell Hall

Bridge No. 189

Bird in the Hand Inn

Bridge No. 88

Snape's Aqueduct

Locks 47 to 52

Bleeding Wolf Inn

Bridge No. 94

Church Lawton

Locks 43/47

Red Bull Aqueduct

KIDSGROVE

Trent & Mersey Canal

Macclesfield Canal

N

Harecastle Tunnel

LITTLE MORTON HALL & TRENT & MERSEY CANAL - 10 miles
- allow 5 hours

◆◆ ◆◆ ◆◆ - *Scholar Green—Macclesfield Canal—Little Morton Hall— Rode Mill— Rode Pool—Rode Heath—Trent & Mersey Canal—Macclesfield Canal— Harecastle Tunnel entrance—Trent & Mersey Canal—Macclesfield Canal—Scholar Green.*

 - *O.S. 1:50,000 Sheet No 118 - The Potteries*
—O.S. 1:25,000 Pathfinder Series Sheet No SJ 85/95
—Kidsgrove and Leek.

🚗 - *No official one at Scholar Green.*
National Trust car park at Little Morton Hall.

🍾 - *Rising Sun Inn, Scholar Green; The Broughton Arms, Rode Heath; Red Bull Inn, Red Bull; Bleeding Wolf Inn, Hall Green.*

ABOUT THE WALK—The longest walks in the book BUT probably the finest canal circuit walk to be done. It is in many ways a GRAND-SLAM of canal features, linking together the Macclesfield and Trent and Mersey canals, seeing locks, aqueducts, the famous Harecastle tunnel, a "two laned" canal (Trent and Mersey) and the "single" laned (Macclesfield) canal and passing the incredible Little Morton Hall. The folly of Mow Cop is always on the horizon, and numerous pubs along the way together with narrow boats passing through the locks, combine to make this a very memorable walk.

WALKING INSTRUCTIONS—Whilst the walk can he started from several locations, such as Red Bull and Rode Heath, I prefer to start from near the Rising Sun Inn, close to the Macclesfield Canal on the north eastern outskirts of Scholar Green. My reason is simply aesthetic, letting the walk unfold in wonder as you progress. Just up from the inn, gain the canal by the righthandside and at the canal left under the bridge. Shortly afterwards pass a canal dock on your right and canal milestone on your left—Marple 25 miles, Hall Green 4 1/4 miles. I/4 mile later pass the imposing Ramsdell Hall on your right, and a further 1/4 mile brings you to a canal bridge and path signs for Little Morton Hall. Here, just before the bridge, leave the canal and turn left, guided by the stile and signs. The path soon joins a track before reaching a stile and path sign. Here you bear right, keeping the hedge on your right. After the second stile you bear left to a stile close to Little Morton Hall. Continue ahead past the Hall and along the drive to the A38 road.

Turn left along the main road for 150 yards to a stile and path sign on your right. Go through the stile and keep beside the hedge on your left to the next stile. Ascend the next field, keeping to the right of Boarded Barn Farm to a track, where bear right to gate, stile and footpath sign. The path line is well signed as you walk around the field edges to pass Moor's Farm. Here you walk along a tarmaced track, bearing left then right on it to pass Rode Mill and gain the minor road—Scholar Green/Rode Heath. Turn right and follow the road round to your left, with Rode Pool in the trees to your left. Keep on the road for almost a mile to the A50 road on the fringe of Rode Heath. Cross and walk along Chapel Lane. At the end gain the A533 road. Turn right along it past Rode Heath Post Office, and just afterwards left in front of The Broughton Arms and cross bridge No 139 over the Trent and Mersey Canal, where turn left onto the canal towpath. You keep on this for the next three miles, crossing Snape's Aqueduct and a whole string of locks—52 to 47—near Church Lawton. After passing under bridge 135 carrying the A50 road you pass another series of locks, to 43—before approaching Pool Aqueduct carrying the Macclesfield canal at Red Bull. Here ascend to the left to the Macclesfield Canal and turn right over the aqueduct, following the Macclesfield Canal to its junction with the Trent and Mersey Canal. Here ascend the bridge No 98 and keep right beside the Trent and Mersey Canal to follow it to the entrance of the Harecastle Tunnel, 1/2 mile away.

Retrace your steps back to bridge 98 and cross it to continue beside the Trent and Mersey Canal past the Bluebell Inn and lock 42. Regain Pool Lock Aqueduct and bear right following the Macclesfield Canal northwards for the next couple of miles back to Scholar Green. In walking order you pass under bridge 94 and further bridges to no 88 just after the Bird in Hand Inn. Just afterwards you approach your starting out path and bridge. Leave the canal here.

LITTLE MORETON HALL - Dating from the 16th century it is a stunning moated manor house and one of the. best examples of black and white design in then country! The property is now cared for by the National Trust and contains an exceptional cobbled courtyard, well tended gardens and numerous rooms rich in carvings, including the long gallery, 68 feet long by 12 feet wide.

Little Moreton Hall.

ACTON AND THE SHROPSHIRE UNION CANAL - 5 miles

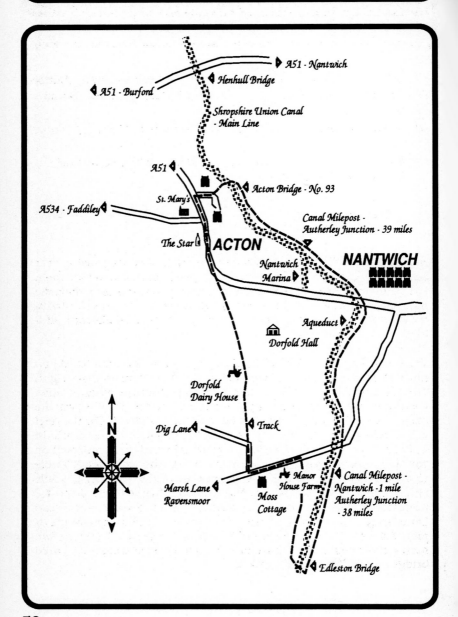

A51 - Nantwich

A51 - Burford

Henhull Bridge

Shropshire Union Canal - Main Line

A51

St. Mary's

A534 - Faddiley

Acton Bridge - No. 93

Canal Milepost - Autherley Junction - 39 miles

The Star

ACTON

NANTWICH

Nantwich Marina

Aqueduct

Dorfold Hall

Dorfold Dairy House

N

Dig Lane

Track

Marsh Lane Ravensmoor

Moss Cottage

Manor House Farm

Canal Milepost - Nantwich - 1 mile Autherley Junction - 38 miles

Edleston Bridge

ACTON AND THE SHROPSHIRE UNION CANAL - 5 miles
- allow 2 hours.

•• •• •• *- Acton - Shropshire Union Canal - Edleston Bridge - Manor House Farm - Marsh Lane - Dig Lane - Dorfold Dairy House - Acton.*

- 0.5. 1:25,000 Pathfinder Series Sheet No 791 (SJ 65/75) Crewe.

- No official one but road side parking in Wilbraham Road. Grid Ref. SJ634534.

- The Star Inn, Acton.

ABOUT THE WALK - An attractive section of canal passing over aqueducts and peaceful countryside despite being close to Nantwich. You return across the Dorfold estate catching glimpses of its majestic hall. Acton church is worth exploring before leaving. Nearby Nantwich is also well worth exploring to see the many excellent timbered buildings.

WALKING INSTRUCTIONS - Starting from Wilbraham Road just north of the church; walk along the road to where it turns sharp right. Turn left past house 33, as footpath signed and a reach a stile. Continue on the well defined path to Acton Bridge (No 93) over the canal. Cross the bridge and turn left and pass under it. For the next 2 1/2 mile keep to the lefthand side of the canal on the towpath. In 1/2 mile pass Nantwich Marina on your right and canal milepost on your left - Autherley Junction 39 miles. In less than another 1/2 mile walk over a splendid aqueduct and continue by the canal. In 3/4 mile reach bridge No 91. Just beyond pass another canal milepost - Nantwich 1 mile/Autherley Junction 38 miles. Pass under Green Lane Bridge No 90 with excellent rope grooves. and in less than 1/2 mile reach the railway bridge and Edleston Bridge No 89. I have often seen a kingfisher in this area. Leave the canal here and cross the canal bridge and railway line via stiles.

Gaining the field cross diagonally to your left to a gate. Continue on a track to another gate, then by a fence on your right to another gate. Through this reach Manor House Farm and exit onto Marsh Lane by another gate. Turn left along the lane passing Moss Cottage on your left. Shortly afterwards turn right into Dig Lane. Where the road turns sharp left continue ahead on a track, footpath signposted - Acton. Pass Dorfold Dairy House on your left and continue on a well defined track for 3/4 mile through Dorfold estate; the hall can be seen to your right close to a wooded lake. Reach the Chester Road in Acton by a path sign- Marsh Lane. Continue ahead past the star Inn, Acton church dedicated to St. Mary, and turn right into Wilbraham Road.

ACTON CHURCH - dedicated to St. Mary it is mostly 13th and 14th century but with earlier stonework. The font is 12th century. Inside are many impressive tombs of the 14th to 16th century especially in the Mainwaring Chapel and to the Wilbraham family.

NANTWICH MARINA - often referred to the "Basin End." The owners of Dorfold Hall objected to their view being spoilt by the canal. Thomas Telford the builder had to make a curve here building a large embankment. The actual marina was the original route of the canal.

DORFOLD HALL - A particularly fine Jacobean building built in 1616 for Ralph Wilbraham. The hall is open to the public on Monday afternoons.

Shropshire Union Canal at Acton Bridge.

Shropshire Union Canal - Aqueduct over Nantwich road.

Moss Cottage.

MOW COP & THE MACCLESFIELD CANAL - 6 miles

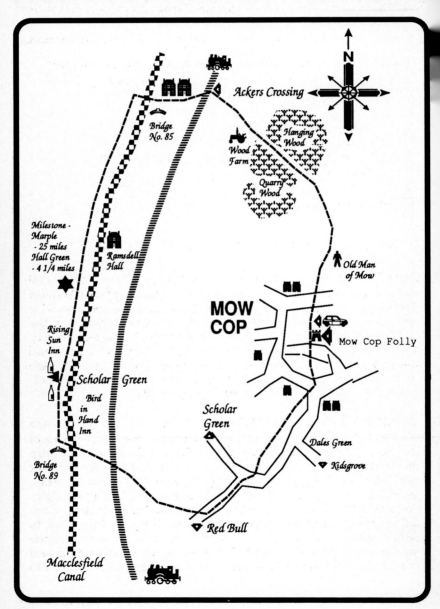

Ackers Crossing

Bridge No. 85

Hanging Wood

Wood Farm

Quarry Wood

Milestone - Marple - 25 miles Hall Green - 4 1/4 miles

Ramsdell Hall

Old Man of Mow

MOW COP

Mow Cop Folly

Rising Sun Inn

Scholar Green

Bird in Hand Inn

Scholar Green

Dales Green

Kidsgrove

Bridge No. 89

Red Bull

Macclesfield Canal

MOW COP & MACCLESFIELD CANAL - 6 miles
-allow 2 1/2 hours.

-*Mow Cop—Dales Green—Bridge No 89—Macclesfield Canal—Ackers Crossing—Roe Park—Hanging Wood—Old Man of Mow—Mow Cop.*

- *O.S. 1:50,000 Sheet No 118 - The Potteries*
  —*O.S. 1:25,000 Pathfinder Series Sheet No SJ 85/95*
  —*Kidsgrove and Leek.*

—*beneath Mow Cop.*

- *Rising Sun Inn and Bird in Hand Inn, Scholar Green.*

ABOUT THE WALK—Dominating the skyline of the southern end of the Macclesfield Canal and adjoining Trent & Mersey Canal is Mow Cop folly. The view from here over the Cheshire Plain and beyond is extensive. Unlike the majority of the walks in this book you start the walk well away from the canal and descend to it. You walk beside it, northwards, for almost two miles passing the Bird in Hand Inn and the attractive Ramsdell Hall. At Ackers Crossing you ascend through particularly unspoilt woodland to regain Mow Cop and the pinnacle of the Old Man of Mow—National Trust property.

WALKING INSTRUCTIONS—The first part of the walk is the hardest to follow, not because the paths are not used but because of the complexity of the area. Basically you keep to the crest of the ridge as you descend and at all junctions keep ahead . From the car park beneath the folly, as guided by the path sign—The Cloud 6 miles—ascend the track to pass directly underneath the folly on your right. Follow the track path around to your right and close to the houses left on the path which soon swings right. Keep on this track to Bellapois House. Here turn left then right immediately and continue on the track for 100 yards before turning left down a path and crossing a new road and housing estate to continue on the path to the next road. Turn right to pass the Hillside Methodist Chapel on your right. A little further turn left onto the track of Rockside Road. Now you begin descending, firstly past several houses before following the spine of the ridge, keeping ahead at all junctions; sometimes a path, sometimes a track. Continue past a quarry on your left before crossing a tarmaced path close to No 45 Rockside. Continue ahead soon to descend into a small rocky dale before gaining the houses of Dales Green. Turn right and follow the road round to your right and after 100 yards take the first road on your left. This is the end of the hard bit!

Continue descending down the road past the 30 mph sign and 200 yards later at the entrance drive to 86 The Hollow, on the left of the entrance is the stile and path. First you head for an electric pole before bearing right to a stile. Beyond is another stile and footbridge. Continue descending gradually to woodland and a stile. The path here is well defined as you walk through the woodland and after 1/4 mile r keep to the righthand path. This soon brings you into the open fields before passing under the railway line. Beyond you bear slightly left to gain Bridge No 89 and the canal. On the otherside of the bridge bear right and right shortly afterwards to reach the towpath.

Turn left and follow the path with the canal on your right. Keep on the canal for almost two miles, passing the Bird in Hand Inn and Ramsdell Hall on your right. At bridge No 85 leave the canal and turn right along the road over the canal into Ackers Crossing.

Follow the road to the righthand bend and turn left along the No Through Road. Cross the railway line and a few yards later gain the track beside the path sign—Mow Cop 1 1/4 miles. Ascend the track bearing right on it at the entrance to Wood Farm. A little further and as guided by signs leave the track to path gate and continue ascending up the field to walk well to the right of the house on your left. At the top lefthand corner of the field is the stile and well defined path. Follow this to your left then right as you continue ascending through woodland. At the end of the wood and near the end of the climb you reach a stile and emerge into open fields. Keep the field boundary on your right as you gently ascend and curve round to your right, passing through several stiles, heading for the pinnacle of the Old Man of Mow. Turn right at the track and shortly afterwards left to pass beneath the pinnacle. At the end of the path bear right then left on a path back to the car park beneath the folly. Again you can savour the view—this time you have earned it!

MOW COP - 1,000 feet above sea level and a magnificent viewpoint over the Cheshire Plain stands the folly known as Mow Cop Castle, built in 1750 by Randle Wilbraham. The summit had a Beacon Tower and was used to signal the Spanish Armada, but has long since gone. Closeby is the rock pinnacle known as the Old Man of Mow Cop and both now belong to the National Trust. A stone beneath the "castle" records the site used in 1807 for the first meeting of the Primitive Methodists. The Staffordshire Way - 92 miles and the Mow Cop Trail start from here.

Macclesfield Canal and Ramsdell Hall

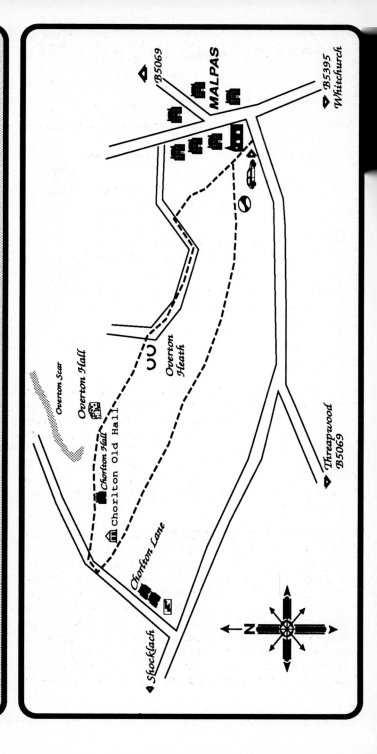

MALPAS AND CHORLTON HALL
- 4 1/2 miles
- allow 2 hours.

- Malpas - Overton Heath - Overton Hall - Chorlton Hall - Chorlton Old Hall - Malpas.

- O.S. 1:25,000 Pathfinder Series sheet No 807 (SJ 44/S4) Whitchurch - (Shropshire) and Malpas (Cheshire).

- No official one. Parking space beside church - Grid Ref. SJ 487473.

- None on walk but several in central Malpas.

ABOUT THE WALK - Starting from high ground views westwards dominate the scene with the Welsh hills around Wrexham in view. Through here runs the Offa's Dyke Footpath. First you cross fields to a bridleway and pass Overton Hall where Cheshire Cheese is still made. Next you cross pleasant fields past Chorlton Hall before passing the magnificent building of Chorlton Old Hall. The paths are little used here but it is all gated. The countryside is quiet with squirrels sitting on gates and barn owls watching you pass. A lovely peaceful walk.

WALKING INSTRUCTIONS - Walk past the church and bear left past the house on your left to a stile. Turn right on a defined path; on your left is the football field and it is around this you will be re-tuning. Follow the path to a stile then beside solitary trees to another stile. Cross a short field beyond to a stile and footpath sign and descend to a lane. Turn left along this and in 1/2 mile where it turns sharp right beside a house on your left, keep straight ahead, as bridlepath signed. The hedged track is overgrown in places in summer and in 1/4 mile pass Overton Hall on your right. There are three gates here to open. Past the hall farm reach a small wooden gate on your left; just ahead is an old quarry and the path beneath Overton Scar.

Go through the gate and keep near a small stream on your left to reach the next gate. Through this aim for the right of Chorlton Hall where there is a stile. Turn right along the drive and in a few yards leave it at the gate on your left. Go diagonally across the field aiming for the lefthand corner of a wood where there is a stile. Cross to another and continue through a large field passing a field corner on your right and keeping to the right of Chorlton Old Hall. Reach a minor road by a stile beside a path sign.

Turn left and left again almost immediately along the drive of Chorlton Old Hall. Keep to the right of the main building to a gate. Continue on a track past a small pond on your right and wood on your left to another gate. Continue with hedge on your left to another gate. The next field is open but You have a track to follow and pass a small sandstone outcrop well to your left. At the end of the field take the righthand gate and keep the fence on your left to another gate. Continue with the fence on your left passing an old square reservoir building on your left and reach another gate. Continue across an open field passing a small pond surrounded by bushes on your right to a wooden fence by an oak tree. Cross this and the subsequent short field to another wooden fence. Cross this and a bridleway to a pole gate. Continue with a hedge on your left to a gate and at the end of the next field another gate. Through this reach a hedged track. Turn right and left after a few yards over a wooden fence close to an electric pole. Cross the field aiming for the righthand corner and another gate - the lefthand one. Cross the corner of the next field to another gate and a few more yards is another gate and football field you saw earlier. The church tower will act as a guide in the final stages. Walk around the football field and reach the stile you crossed at the beginning and regain the church.

OVERTON HALL - Parties of ten or more can visit the farmhouse and see real Cheshire Cheese made. Access is by road and not via the footpath. Tel. 0948-860519. The famous Cheshire Cheeses includes white Cheshire, red Cheshire and the special "old blue."

MALPAS - The church dedicated to St. Oswald is mostly 14th and 15th century and built from red sandstone. Inside are many monuments to the Cholmondeley and Brereton families. If time permits the town is worth exploring to see mediaeval buildings, old inns and almshouses.

Track and Overton Hall on left.

Chorlton Old Hall.

AUDLEM & THE SHROPSHIRE UNION CANAL - 4 miles

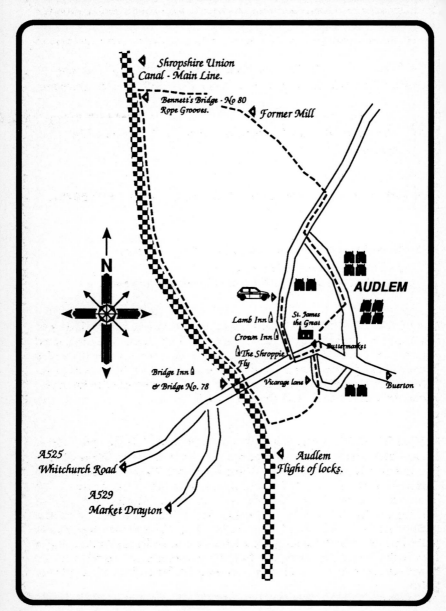

Shropshire Union Canal - Main Line.

Bennett's Bridge - No 80
Rope Grooves.

Former Mill

N

AUDLEM

St. James
the Great

Lamb Inn

Crown Inn

Buttermarket

The Shroppie
Fly

Bridge Inn
& Bridge No. 78

Vicarage lane

Buerton

A525
Whitchurch Road

Audlem
Flight of locks.

A529
Market Drayton

AUDLEM & THE SHROPSHIRE UNION CANAL - 4 miles
- allow 2 hours.

•➤ •➤ •➤ *- Audlem - Audlem Locks & Wharf - Shropshire Union Canal Bennett's Bridge - Weaver Mill - Little Heath - Audlem.*

- 0.5. 1:25,000 Pathfinder Series Sheet No 808 (SJ 64/74) Audlem.

- on Cheshire street - the A529 road. Grid Ref. SJ 659437.

- Several in central Audlem including the Lamb Inn, Lord Combermere and Crown Inn. At Audlem Wharf is the Shroppie Fly ~and Bridge Inn.

ABOUT THE WALK - Audlem is a particularly interesting and attractive place and well worth exploring while here. The walk itself is stunning with the Audlem Locks and wharf. You explore two miles of the Shropshire Union Canal before crossing the fields and passing a former mill back to Audlem. On the way through the town you can visit the church and Buttermarket.

WALKING INSTRUCTIONS - Turn right out of the car park along Cheshire Street to the Buttermarket. Turn left then right almost immediately and walk down Vicarage Lane. Where the lane turns right bear right to a stile followed by another. After this one turn right and walk close to the stream on your right through the Vale of Audlem. In 200 yards you begin ascending to a stile and the Shropshire Union Canal. Turn right along the towpath but if time Permits it is worth turning left to explore more fully the Audlem flight of locks. Continue along the towpath passing under Bridge No 78 with the Bridge Inn. Just after is Audlem Wharf and the Shroppie Fly Inn.

Continue on the towpath soon passing a canal milepost on your right - Nantwich 6 miles/Autherley Junction 33 miles. A short distance later Pass under Moss Hall Bridge - you can just glimpse the hall from the towpath. Continue on the towpath with the canal on your left for a further mile to Bridge No 80 - Bennett's Bridge. There are some really excellent rope grooves here. Leave the canal here and gain a small gate. Follow the track away from the canal to the first gate on your right. Keep to the lefthand side of the field to another gate. through this on your left is the wooden stile. Keep the fence on your right as you walk along the field edge to the next stile. Continue ahead now on a track and cross the River Weaver and former mill on your left. At the end of the building turn right at the stile and ascend the valley side and pass close to a tall hedge on your left. Beyond you descend slightly to a stile and wooden footbridge across a stream. Continue ascending gently to a wooden fence - no stile here. Cross the next field aiming for the righthand side of a row of houses. Here is a stile, footbridge and path sign.

Turn right and in a few yards turn left into Heathfield Road - on your right is a large grass triangle. Follow the road for the next 1/4 mile, passing the school. Turn right into Hillary Drive and at the end turn left into Church View. Turn right immediately onto the signed footpath and at its end left between the houses to the Buttermarket. Turn right past the church to Cheshire Street and just up here on your left is the car park.

AUDLEM - The church dedicated to St. James The Great dates from 1278 but much of it 14th and 17th century workmanship. In front of the church is the Buttermarket built in 1733; the charter for the market dates back to 1296 and a market was held here until early this century. Close to the church gate is the bear stone that once stood in the middle of the square. Bear baiting was once a popular feature of village life.

SHROPSHIRE UNION CANAL - Today the main canal from Elles-mere Port to Autherley Junction and its side branches total 158 miles of canal. The section here from Autherley Junction of Nantwich - 39 miles - was engineered by Thomas Telford. Work began in 1826 and was completed in 1835. Upto early this century the Audlem Wharf was a busy scene with goods being loaded onto boats, especially cheese. The Audlem Flight of 15 locks lowers the canal 93 feet and takes a narrowboat more than two hours to make the ascent or descent.

MOSS HALL - Although only glimpsed from the canal, the Elizabe-than timber framed manor house was built about 1616.

Shropshire Union Canal - Audlem Flight.

The Shroppie Fly Inn, Audlem.

REMEMBER AND OBSERVE THE COUNTRY CODE

 Enjoy the countryside and respect its life and work.

 Guard against all risk of fire.

Fasten all gates.

 Keep your dogs under close control.

 Keep to public paths across farmland.

Use gates and stiles to cross fences, hedges and walls.

 Leave livestock, crops and machinery alone.

 Take your litter home - pack it in; pack it out.

Help to keep all water clean.

 Protect wildlife, plants and trees.

 Take special care on country roads.

THE HIKER'S CODE

❀ *Hike only along marked routes - do not leave the trail.*

❀ *Use stiles to climb fences; close gates.*

❀ *Camp only in designated campsites.*

❀ *Carry a light-weight stove.*

❀ *Leave the trail cleaner than you found it.*

❀ *Leave flowers and plants for others to enjoy.*

❀ *Keep dogs on a leash.*

❀ *Protect and do not disturb wildlife.*

❀ *Use the trail at your own risk.*

❀ *Leave only your thanks and footprints - take nothing but photographs.*

EQUIPMENT NOTES

Some personal

thoughts

BOOTS - *preferably with a full leather upper, of medium weight, with a vibram sole. I always add a foam cushioned insole to help cushion the base of my feet.*

SOCKS - *I generally wear two thick pairs as this helps minimise blisters. The inner pair are of loop stitch variety and approximately 80% wool. The outer are a thick rib pair of approximately 80% wool.*

WATERPROOFS - *for general walking I wear a T shirt or cotton shirt with a cotton wind jacket on top. You generate heat as you walk and I prefer to layer my clothes to avoid getting too hot. Depending on the season will dictate how many layers you wear. In soft rain I just use my wind jacket for I know it quickly dries out. In heavy or consistant rain I slip on a neoprene lined gagoule, and although hot and clammy it does keep me reasonably dry. Only in extreme conditions will I don overtrousers, much preferring to get wet and feel comfortable. I never wear gaiters!*

FOOD - *as I walk I carry bars of chocolate, for they provide instant energy and are light to carry. In winter a flask of hot coffee is welcome. I never carry water and find no hardship from not doing so, but this is a personal matter! From experience I find the more I drink the more I want and sweat. You should always carry some extra food such as Kendal Mint Cake, for emergencies.*

RUCKSACKS - *for day walking I use a climbing rucksack of about 40 litre capacity and although it leaves excess space it does mean that the sac is well padded, with an internal frame and padded shoulder straps. Inside apart from the basics for one day I carry gloves, balaclava, spare pullover and a pair of socks.*

MAP & COMPASS - *when I am walking I always have the relevant map - preferably 1:25,000 scale - open in my hand. This enables me to constantly check that I am walking the right way. In case of bad weather I carry a compass, which once mastered gives you complete confidence in thick cloud or mist.*

WALK RECORD CHART

DATE WALKED

BEACON HILL & HELSBY HILL – 8 miles...............⬭

LYME PARK & BOW STONES – 4 miles....................⬭

DELAMERE FOREST – 6 miles..............................⬭

ANDERTON & TRENT & MERSEY CANAL – 3 miles..⬭

ALDERLEY EDGE – 6 miles..................................⬭

LOWER PEOVER & PEOVER HALL – 7 miles..............⬭

BEESTON & WASTE HILL – 4 1/2 miles....................⬭

BICKERTON HILL & BULKELEY HILL – 4 1/2 miles...⬭

BICKERTON & MAIDEN CASTLE – 3 miles...............⬭

SANDBACH & TRENT & MERSEY CANAL – 5 1/2 miles..⬭

LITTLE MORETON HALL – 10 miles.........................⬭

NANTWICH & SHROPSHIRE UNION CANAL – 5 miles.⬭

MOW COP & MACCLESFIELD CANAL – 6 miles.........⬭

MALPAS & CHORLTON HALL – 4 1/2 miles...............⬭

AUDLEM & SHROPSHIRE UNION CANAL – 4 miles....⬭

THE JOHN MERRILL WALK BADGE

Complete six of the walks in this book and get the above special walk badge. Badges are a black cloth with walking man embroidered in four colours and measure - 3 1/2" in diameter.

BADGE ORDER FORM

Date and details of walks completed ....

....

NAME ....

ADDRESS ....

....

Price: £2.00 each including postage, VAT and signed completion certificate.
Amount enclosed (Payable to JNM Publications) ....
From: JNM PUBLICATIONS, Winster, Matlock, Derbyshire. DE4 2DQ.

✆ Winster (062988) 454 - 24hr answering service.
FAX: Winster (062988) 416

************* YOU MAY PHOTOCOPY THIS FORM *************

OTHER BOOKS by JOHN N. MERRILL PUBLISHED by JNM PUBLICATIONS

CIRCULAR WALK GUIDES -
SHORT CIRCULAR WALKS IN THE PEAK DISTRICT
LONG CIRCULAR WALKS IN THE PEAK DISTRICT
CIRCULAR WALKS IN WESTERN PEAKLAND
SHORT CIRCULAR WALKS IN THE STAFFORDSHIRE MOORLANDS
SHORT CIRCULAR WALKS AROUND THE TOWNS & VILLAGES OF
THE PEAK DISTRICT
SHORT CIRCULAR WALKS AROUND MATLOCK
SHORT CIRCULAR WALKS IN THE DUKERIES
SHORT CIRCULAR WALKS IN SOUTH YORKSHIRE
SHORT CIRCULAR WALKS AROUND DERBY
SHORT CIRCULAR WALKS AROUND BUXTON
SHORT CIRCULAR WALKS IN THE HOPE VALLEY
40 SHORT CIRCULAR WALKS IN THE PEAK DISTRICT
CIRCULAR WALKS ON KINDER & BLEAKLOW
SHORT CIRCULAR WALKS IN SOUTH NOTTINGHAMSHIRE
SHIRT CIRCULAR WALKS IN CHESHIRE

CANAL WALKS -
VOL 1 - DERBYSHIRE & NOTTINGHAMSHIRE
VOL 2 - CHESHIRE & STAFFORDSHIRE
VOL 3 - STAFFORDSHIRE
VOL 4 - THE CHESHIRE RING
VOL 5 - LINCOLNSHIRE & NOTTINGHAMSHIRE
VOL 6 - SOUTH YORKSHIRE
VOL 7 - THE TRENT & MERSEY CANAL

JOHN MERRILL DAY CHALLENGE WALKS -
WHITE PEAK CHALLENGE WALK
DARK PEAK CHALLENGE WALK
PEAK DISTRICT END TO END WALKS
STAFFORDSHIRE MOORLANDS CHALLENGE WALK
THE LITTLE JOHN CHALLENGE WALK
YORKSHIRE DALES CHALLENGE WALK
NORTH YORKSHIRE MOORS CHALLENGE WALK
LAKELAND CHALLENGE WALK

INSTRUCTION & RECORD -
HIKE TO BE FIT.....STROLLING WITH JOHN
THE JOHN MERRILL WALK RECORD BOOK

MULTIPLE DAY WALKS -
THE RIVERS'S WAY
PEAK DISTRICT: HIGH LEVEL ROUTE
PEAK DISTRICT MARATHONS
THE LIMEY WAY
THE PEAKLAND WAY

COAST WALKS & NATIONAL TRAILS -
ISLE OF WIGHT COAST PATH
PEMBROKESHIRE COAST PATH
THE CLEVELAND WAY

PEAK DISTRICT HISTORICAL GUIDES -
DERBYSHIRE INNS - an A to Z guide
HALLS AND CASTLES OF THE PEAK DISTRICT & DERBYSHIRE
TOURING THE PEAK DISTRICT & DERBYSHIRE BY CAR
DERBYSHIRE FOLKLORE
PUNISHMENT IN DERBYSHIRE
CUSTOMS OF THE PEAK DISTRICT & DERBYSHIRE
WINSTER - a souvenir guide
ARKWRIGHT OF CROMFORD
TALES FROM THE MINES by Geoffrey Carr
PEAK DISTRICT PLACE NAMES by Martin Spray

JOHN MERRILL'S MAJOR WALKS -
TURN RIGHT AT LAND'S END
WITH MUSTARD ON MY BACK
TURN RIGHT AT DEATH VALLEY
EMERALD COAST WALK

COLOUR GUIDES -
THE PEAK DISTRICT.........Something to remember her by.

SKETCH BOOKS -
NORTH STAFFORDSHIRE SKETCHBOOK by John Creber

IN PREPARATION -
LONG CIRCULAR WALKS IN STAFFORDSHIRE
SHORT CIRCULAR WALKS IN WEST YORKSHIRE
SHORT CIRCULAR WALKS IN THE YORKSHIRE DALES
SHORT CIRCULAR WALKS IN THE LAKE DISTRICT
SHORT CIRCULAR WALKS IN NORTH YORKSHIRE MOORS
RUTLAND WATER CHALLENGE WALK
SNOWDONIA CHALLENGE WALK
FOOTPATHS OF THE WORLD - Vol 1 - NORTH AMERICA
HIKING IN NEW MEXICO

☞ Full list from JNM PUBLICATIONS, Winster, Matlock, Derbys.